Dhimmi - Non Muslims Living in the Khilafah

Abdul-Kareem Newell

Translation of the Qur'ān

It should be perfectly clear that the Qur'ān is only authentic in its original language, Arabic. Since perfect translation of the Qur'ān is impossible, we have used the translation of the meaning of the Qur'ān throughout the book, as the result is only a crude meaning of the Arabic text.

Qur'ānic verses appear in speech marks proceeded by a reference to the Surah and verse number. Sayings (*Hadith*) of Prophet Muhammad ﷺ appear in inverted commas along with reference to the Hadith Book and its Reporter.

(Peace be upon him) ﷺ - صلى الله عليه وسلم

(Glory to Him, the Exalted) ﷻ - سبحانه وتعالى

2

Contents

Introduction

The position of non-Muslims living under Islamic rule (*dhimmi*) is a widely misunderstood topic. Those wishing to attack Islam and its systems portray Islam's treatment of the *dhimmi* as worse than its treatment of animals. Historical incidents where *dhimmi* suffered persecution at particular times are generalized and quoted out of context in order to back up their claims.

Joseph Farah, founder of the WorldNetDaily news site states: Under Islamic *Shari'ah* law, non-believers – Christians and Jews anyway – are permitted to live as long as they support Islam through their *Dhimmi* taxes and are willing to accept what amounts to a third- or fourth-class servile existence, always subject to pogroms, false accusations and ill treatment. *Dhimmi*s always live in fear.[1]

Melanie Philips, prominent UK based Zionist author and commentator states: '*Dhimmi*' is the status of infidels under Islam who are permitted to live in Muslim jurisdictions but only with restrictions as second-class citizens.[2]

To answer this accusation that *dhimmi* are second-class citizens who will have a miserable existence living in a future Khilafah we need to look at Islam's view on citizenship and how it applies to non-Muslims.

Citizenship in Islam

Citizenship in Islam is based on someone permanently living within the lands of the Khilafah regardless of their ethnicity or creed. It is not a requirement for someone to become Muslim and adopt the values of Islam in order to become a citizen of the state. Muslims living outside the Islamic State do not enjoy the rights of citizenship, whereas a non-Muslim living permanently within the Islamic State (dar ul-Islam) does. This is derived from the following hadith.

The Prophet (saw) said: 'Call them to Islam, and if they agree accept from them and refrain from fighting against them, then call them to move from their land to the land of the *Muhajireen* (the emigrants), and tell them if they do so, then they will have the rights which the *Muhajireen* enjoy and they will have duties like the duties upon the *Muhajireen.*'[3]

This hadith means if they do not move to the land of the *Muhajireen* they would not enjoy what the *Muhajireen* enjoy, i.e. the rights of those who are living in the land of Islam. So this Hadith clearly shows the difference between those who move to the land of the *Muhajireen* and those who do not move to the land of the *Muhajireen*. Dar ul-*Muhajireen* was the land of Islam (Dar ul-Islam) at the time of the Prophet (saw), and all other lands were Dar ul-Kufr.[4]

The Islamic state is forbidden from discriminating between citizens on the basis of race, creed, colour or anything else. In origin all the rules of Islam apply equally to Muslims and non-Muslims. The Islamic scholars have agreed, especially the scholars of *Usul* (foundations), that the divine rules are addressed to every sane person able to understand the speech, whether he is Muslim or not, male or female.[5]

However, there are exceptions to this. If the *Shari'ah* rule is dependent on belief in Islam such as praying salah or giving the zakat tax then it applies only to Muslims. These exceptions are not discriminatory rules as some have claimed, but take in to account the beliefs and values of the citizen so as not to cause oppression to them. They in no way detract from being equal citizens.

Categories of non-Muslims in the Khilafah

There are four main categories of non-Muslims in the Khilafah. These are:

1. *Mu'ahid*
2. Must'amin
3. Ambassadors, diplomats, consuls and envoys
4. *Dhimmi*

The *Mu'ahid* is a citizen of a foreign state with which the Khilafah has a treaty. The citizens of this state (*mu'ahid*een) can enter the Khilafah without a passport or visa if this is reciprocated to the citizens of the Khilafah.[6]

The Must'amin is a citizen of a foreign state with which the Khilafah has no treaty. These states are the imperialistic states such as Britain, America, Russia and France. The citizens of these states can enter the Khilafah but only with a passport and valid visa. Once they have received a valid visa and enter the state they are termed Must'amin.[7]

If the *Mu'ahid* or Must'amin stays for more than one year within the Khilafah then their stay is considered permanent and they are required to pay the *jizya* (head tax) and will become *dhimmi*.[8]

When discussing the rights and responsibilities of the *dhimmi* in this article these for the most part apply equally to both the *Mu'ahid* and the Must'amin. The exceptions are in the specific terms of the treaties and visa applications adopted by the Khaleefah.

The Ambassadors, diplomats, consuls and envoys from the foreign states have diplomatic immunity and the rules of Islam do not apply on them.[9]

The *dhimmi*

Dhimmi are those citizens of the Khilafah that hold different beliefs and values to the ideology of the state i.e. Islam. The word *dhimmi* is derived from the Arabic word dhimmah, which means pledge or covenant ('ahd).[10]

The state makes a pledge to treat the *dhimmi* in accordance with the specific terms of the peace treaty made with them (if applicable) and not to interfere in their beliefs, worships and those actions that contradict Islam but were permitted to the *dhimmi* by the Messenger of Allah (saw) such as drinking alcohol. In all other areas they are viewed and treated in the same way as Muslims unless belief in Islam is a condition for the action.

There are many ahadith ordering good treatment of the *dhimmi* and not abusing them or treating them as second-class citizens.

The Messenger of Allah (saw) said: "He who harms a person under covenant, or charged him more than he can, I will argue against him on the Day of Judgement."[11]

The Messenger of Allah (saw) said: "He who hurts a dhimmi hurts me, and he who hurts me annoys Allah."[12]

The classical scholars of Islam also detailed the rights of the Muslims towards the *dhimmi*. The famous Maliki jurist, Shaha al-Deen al-Qarafi states:

The covenant of protection imposes upon us certain obligations toward the ahl al-dhimmah. They are our neighbours, under our shelter and protection upon the guarantee of Allah, His Messenger (saw), and the religion of Islam. Whoever violates these obligations against any one of them by so much as an abusive word, by slandering his reputation, or by doing him some injury or assisting in it, has breached the guarantee of Allah, His Messenger (saw), and the religion of Islam.[13]

Judiciary

One of the accusations against Islam's treatment of *dhimmi* is that a *dhimmi* is not allowed to give evidence against a Muslim and his oath is not acceptable in an Islamic court.

Bat Ye'or states: Every legal case involving a Muslim and a *dhimmi* was judged according to Koranic law. Although the very idea of justice implies equality between parties, a *dhimmi* was not allowed to give evidence against a Muslim. Since his oath was unacceptable in an Islamic court his Muslim opponent could not easily be condemned. In order to defend himself, the *dhimmi* was obliged to purchase Muslim witnesses at great expense.[14]

The rule of law applies to everyone within the Khilafah and there are no exceptions. It is obligatory for the Islamic State to judge in cases concerning the *dhimmi* with justice and no discrimination against them is allowed.

Allah (swt) says in the Holy Qur'an: *"And if you judge, judge with justice between them. Verily, Allah loves those who act justly."*[15]

The most famous example of this justice is in the legal trial of a Jew who stole the coat of armour of Imam Ali (ra) as he was travelling to a battle. The judge Shurayh made no exception for Ali (ra) even though he was the Khaleefah, a Muslim and also off to fight in a battle so was in desperate need of his armour. Shurayh ruled in favour of the Jew and accepted his testimony in court. Full details of the trial can be read here.

The *dhimmi* is allowed to be a witness in an Islamic court against a Muslim and their evidence is acceptable. The conditions of being a witness apply equally to Muslims and *dhimmi*. The conditions of a witness are: sane, mature and 'adl (trustworthy).

It may be claimed that the condition of 'Adl applies only to Muslims who refrain from committing the kabeera (major) sins. This is incorrect. 'Adl in this context means someone who abstains from that which the people consider a violation of uprightness, whether he was a Muslim or non-Muslim. This is because 'adaala (trustworthiness) was stipulated in the testimony of the Muslim as well as in the testimony of the non-Muslim, by using the same word without distinguishing one from the other.

Allah (swt) says in the Holy Qur'an: *"O you who believe! Let there be witnesses between you when death draws to one of you, at the time of bequest, two witnesses, 'adl (trustworthy) from among you, or two others from other than you".*[16]

He (swt) meant non-Muslims by saying other than you. He said 'two 'adl witnesses from Muslims or two 'adl from other than Muslims.' So how can the 'adaala be defined as not committing a kabeera (major) sin and insistence on committing a sagheera (small) sin regarding a non-Muslim? Also how can we reject as a witness the one who disobeyed his parents once, but accept as witness the spy, just because spying is not from kabeera sins? Therefore, the valid meaning of 'adl is the one that abstained from that which the people consider violation to the uprightness.[17]

Criminal punishments

Another accusation is that Muslims are given a lesser punishment for crimes against *dhimmi*. In the case of murder it is alleged that a Muslim is not killed for the murder of a *dhimmi* whereas a *dhimmi* is killed for the murder of a Muslim. Bat Ye'or states: The punishment that a guilty Muslim received for a crime would be greatly reduced if the victim were a *dhimmi*.[18]

Again this is a false accusation. Punishments for crimes are applied equally to both Muslims and *dhimmi* with no distinction. The only distinction is that *dhimmi* will not be punished for those actions which are permitted for them such as drinking alcohol, whereas a Muslim would be.

The Prophet (saw) said, "The *diyyah* (blood money) of the Jews and Christians is like the Muslim's *diyyah*."[19]

It is narrated in a hadith, "that the Messenger of Allah (saw) killed a Muslim for a *mu'ahid* and said, 'I am the most noble of those who fulfil their dhimmah'."[20]

This hadith clearly indicates that if a Muslim kills a *mu'ahid* he is punished with death.[21] This equally applies to the killing of a *dhimmi* as discussed earlier.

Economy

The *dhimmi* enjoy the same economic benefits as Muslims. They can be employees, establish companies, be partners with Muslims and buy and sell goods. Their wealth is protected and if they are poor and unable to find work they are entitled to state benefits from the Khilafah's Treasury (Bait ul-Mal).

Historically, many *dhimmi* prospered within the lands of the Khilafah.

Cecil Roth mentions that the treatment of the Jews at the hands of the Ottoman State attracted Jews from all over Western Europe. The land of Islam became the land of opportunity. Jewish physicians from the school of Salanca were employed in the service of the Sultan and the Viziers (ministers). In many places glass making and metalworking were Jewish monopolies, and with their knowledge of foreign languages, they were the greatest competitors of the Venetian traders.[22]

The poor *dhimmi* will receive state benefits if they are in need.

'Umar ibn al-Khattab once passed by an old *dhimmi* begging at doors, and said: "We have not done justice to you if we have taken *jizya* from you in the prime of your youth and neglected you in your old age." He then ordered from the treasury what was suitable for him.[23]

With regards taxation the *Shari'ah* has put the condition of belief on some of the taxes, which means they are applied differently between the Muslims and *dhimmi*. Muslims for example are ordered to pay the Zakat but *dhimmi* are exempt, whereas *dhimmi* are ordered to pay the *jizya* (head tax) but Muslims are exempt.

Jizya

The most misunderstood Islamic taxation is the *jizya*. Some historians paint a picture that the *jizya* tax was so high that *dhimmi* were forced to convert to Islam to avoid it. Others bring out arbitrary *jizya* rates such as 50%.[24]

The obligation of the *jizya* is derived from the following verse of the Qur'an.

Allah (swt) says: *Fight those who believe not in Allah nor the Last Day, nor hold forbidden that which hath been forbidden by Allah and His Messenger, nor acknowledge the religion of Truth, (even if they are) of the People of the Book, until they pay the Jizyah with willing submission, and feel themselves subdued (saghiroon).*[25]

The 'subdued' (sighar) mentioned in this verse means the *dhimmi* must submit to the rules of Islam. It does not mean physical humiliation.[26]

The *jizya* tax is applied to all mature, male *dhimmi* who have the means to pay it. Women and children are exempt as are the poor who have no livelihood.[27]

The *jizya* is applied according to the prosperity of the *dhimmi*. In the time of 'Umar ibn al-Khattab (ra) he established three different bands of *jizya* depending on the prosperity of the person. The *jizya* rates for different provinces (wiliyat) of the Khilafah in the time of 'Umar ibn al-Khattab (ra) is shown below.

Yemen[28]

	Dinars	Weight of dinar in grams	Grams in gold
Everyone eligible	1	4.25	4.25

Iraq[29]

	Dirhams silver coin	Weight of dirhams in grams	Grams in silver
The rich	48	2.975	142.80
The middle class	24	2.975	71.4
The worker	12	2.975	35.7

Eqypt & Ash-Sham[30]

	Dinars (gold coins)	Weight of dinar in grams	Grams in gold
The rich	4	4.25	17 grams
The middle class	2	4.25	8.50 grams
The worker	1	4.25	4.25 grams

In sahih Bukhari it has been narrated by Abu Najeeh who said, "I said to Mujahid: 'What is the matter with the people of Ash-Sham who pay 4 Dinars and the people of Yemen pay 1 Dinar?' He said, 'This was decided based on prosperity.'"[31]

It is forbidden for the Khilafah to overburden the *dhimmi* with heavy taxation.

The Messenger of Allah (saw) said: "He who harms a person under covenant, or charged him more than he can, I will argue against him on the Day of Judgement."[32]

'Amr ibn Maymun said, "I saw 'Umar four nights before he was assassinated sitting on top a camel, saying to Hudhayfa ibn al-Yaman and 'Uthman ibn al-Hunayf, 'Review the affairs under your charge. Do you think that you have burdened the tenants with what they cannot bear?" 'Uthman replied, 'I have levied on them an amount that I could double and they would still have the ability to pay.' Hudhayfa said: 'I have imposed on them an amount that leaves a large surplus.'"

Abu Ubayd commenting on this said: this is the legal rule in our view for the imposition of *jizya* and kharaj; they are levied in accordance with the capacity of the *dhimmi*s to pay, without burdening them and without adversely affecting the fay' of the Muslims; however, no limit is imposed on it.[33]

When collecting the *jizya* this cannot be collected by abusing and torturing the *dhimmi* as some have claimed.

It is narrated from Hisham bin Hakeem, who said; "I bear witness that I heard the Messenger of Allah (saw) say;

'Allah will punish those who punish the people in the Dunya.'"[34]

'Umar ibn al-Khattab was brought a huge amount of wealth – Abu Ubayd: I believe, he said "Of *jizya*" – and he ('Umar) said: "I think you must have placed the people in hardship (for such wealth)." They said: "No, by Allah, we did not collect anything that was not given voluntarily and of their own free will." He said: "Without using the stick and without stringing (them

18

up).” They said: “Yes.” He said: “Praise be to Allah, who has not caused this to happen at my hands or during my authority.” [35]

With regards the Kharaj (agricultural land tax) this applies equally to Muslims and *dhimmi* with no distinction.

Community relations

Muslim and *dhimmi* communities live together, side by side in the Khilafah. They are not persecuted, hated and forced to live in fear by the Muslims.

The *dhimmi* neighbours have the same rights as Muslim neighbours with no distinction.

The Prophet (saw) said: "Jibril (Angel Gabriel) kept recommending treating neighbours with kindness until I thought he would assign them a share of inheritance."[36]

Muslims and *dhimmi* will visit each other, be courteous and socialise together. The Messenger of Allah (saw) used to visit the poorly from amongst the *dhimmi*.

It is narrated that a Jewish valet who used to serve the Messenger of Allah (saw) was once taken ill, so the Messenger of Allah (saw) visited him.[37]

Thomas Arnold describes the relations between *dhimmi* and Muslim communities in Spain under Islamic rule.

The toleration of the Muhammadan government towards its Christian subjects in Spain and the freedom of intercourse between the adherents of the two religions brought about a certain amount of assimilation in the two communities. Inter-marriages became frequent; Isidore of Beja, who fiercely inveighs against the Muslim conquerors, records the marriage of 'Abd al-Aziz, the son of Musa, with the widow of King Roderic, without a word of blame. Many of the Christians adopted Arab names, and in outward observances imitated to some extent their Muhammadan neighbours, e.g. many were circumcised, and in matters of food and drink followed the practice of the "unbaptized pagans.[38]

The Christian Arabs of the present day, dwelling in the midst of a Muhammadan population, are a living testimony of this toleration; Layard speaks of having come across an encampment of Christian Arabs at al-Karak, to the east of the Dead Sea, who differed in no way either in dress or in manners, from the Muslim Arabs.[39]

Government

Another accusation is that *dhimmi* cannot be civil servants within the Khilafah or be members of the government. It's true that a *dhimmi* cannot hold any ruling position within the Khilafah. This is because the *Shari'ah* has restricted these positions to those who believe in the ideology of the state i.e. Islam. This is no different to any ideological state within the world today.

Muhammad Asad states:
One cannot escape the fact that no non-Muslim citizen – however great his personal integrity and his loyalty to the state – could, on psychological grounds, ever be supposed to work wholeheartedly for the ideological objectives of Islam; nor, in fairness, could such a demand be made of him. On the other hand, no ideological organization (whether based on religious or other doctrines) can afford to entrust the direction of its affairs to persons not professing its ideology. Is it, for instance, conceivable that a non-Communist could be given a political key position – not to speak of supreme leadership of the state – in Soviet Russia? Obviously not, and logically so: for as long as communism supplies the ideological basis of the state, only persons who identify themselves unreservedly with its aims can be relied upon to translate those aims into terms of administrative policy.[40]

Having said this *dhimmi* can be civil servants and directors of the administrative government departments. Discrimination against *dhimmi* for civil service posts is forbidden.

The evidence for this is from the Islamic rules on hiring (Ijara) where it is permitted to hire any person whether Muslim or non-Muslim. This is because the evidences for hiring came in a general form.

Allah (swt) says; *And if they suckled for you, do give them their wage.*[41]

The Messenger of Allah (saw) said: "Allah (swt) said; I will challenge three people on the day of Judgement..... and a man who employed a labourer, he received from him (the work) but did not give him his wage."[42]

The Messenger of Allah (saw) himself once hired a man from the tribe Banu Ad-Deel who was a non-Muslim, which indicates that it is permitted to hire a non-Muslim just as it is to hire a Muslim.

All the above three evidences are general. Therefore, it is permitted for a non-Muslim to be a director of a government department or an employee in that department, for they are all hired staff, and the evidences about hiring are general.[43]

Although *dhimmi* cannot hold ruling positions within the government this does not mean they cannot politically participate within the Khilafah.

One of the pillars of the Islamic ruling system is consultation (shura). This function is institutionalised within an elected council called the Majlis al-Ummah (Council of the Ummah) that forms part of the Khilafah government.

The Majlis al-Ummah is an elected council whose members can be Muslim, non-Muslim, men or women. These members represent the interests of their constituencies within the state. The majlis has no powers of legislation like in a democratic parliament but it does have many powers that act as a counterbalance to the executive powers of the Khaleefah.

Members of the majlis can voice their political opinions freely without fear of imprisonment or rebuke. This makes the Majlis ul-Ummah a very

23

powerful institution for accounting the Khaleefah and his government that the *dhimmi* can fully participate in.[44]

Religion

A widespread accusation against the Khilafah is that Islam was spread by the sword forcing non-Muslims to convert to Islam or die. This claim in particular is used to create fear and opposition within western countries to the re-emergence of a Khilafah in the Muslim world.

Islam categorically forbids forcing anyone to convert to Islam.

Allah (swt) says: *"Let there be no compulsion in religion"* [45]

Thomas Arnold states: The toleration extended towards the Christian Arabs by the victorious Muslims of the first century of the Hijrah and continued by succeeding generations, we may surely infer that those Christian tribes that did embrace Islam, did so of their own choice and free will. [46]

Islam has also forbidden tempting non-Muslims away from their beliefs and worships. The Messenger of Allah (saw) wrote to the people of Yemen:

'Whoever is adamant upon Judaism or Christianity will not be tormented for it, and he is obliged to pay the *jizya.*' [47]

The meaning of 'will not be tormented for it' means the *dhimmi* are left to follow their beliefs and worships. [48] Therefore *dhimmi* are allowed to follow their own beliefs, the rules of their religion and perform actions with although forbidden in Islam were permitted to them by the Messenger of Allah (saw) such as drinking alcohol, eating pork, marriage and divorce. [49]

The *dhimmi* places of worship are also protected by the Khilafah. The existence of centuries old Churches, Synagogues and Temples throughout the Muslim world is clear evidence to this fact.

Since these areas are the only areas a religion such as Christianity, Judaism or Hinduism has detailed rules for, the *dhimmi* will generally face no conflicts between their religions and living within the Khilafah.

Conclusion

The *dhimmi* are citizens of the Khilafah and enjoy all the rights of citizenship such as protection, guaranteed living and fair treatment. They also enjoy the right of being treated with kindness, leniency, justice and clemency. They can join the Islamic armed forces and fight alongside the Muslims if they choose to do so, but they are not obliged to fight as the Muslims are. They are viewed by the ruler and the judge in the same light as the Muslims are viewed without any discrimination in terms of managing their affairs and when implementing the rules of transactions (mu'amilat) and the penal code (*hudud*) upon them.

Therefore, the *dhimmi* enjoys all the rights, equally and exactly as those enjoyed by the Muslims and is in no way classed as a second class citizen.[50]

References

[1] Joseph Farah, October 26, 2006, Between the Lines Commentary, http://www.worldnetdaily.com/news/article.asp?ARTICLE_ID=52609

[2] Melanie Phillips, '*Dhimmi* Britain,' January 14, 2004, http://www.melaniephillips.com/diary/archives/000265.html

[3] Narrated by Sulayman Bin Buraida, Sahih Muslim, Hadith no. 4294

[4] Hizb ut-Tahrir, 'The Methodology of Hizb ut-Tahrir for Change,' Al-Khilafah Publications, p. 6

[5] Taqiuddin an-Nabhani, 'The Ruling System in Islam,' translation of Nizam ul-Hukm fil Islam, Khilafah Publications, Fifth Edition, p. 247

[6] Taqiuddin an-Nabhani, 'The draft constitution of the Khilafah State. The Introduction and the incumbent reasons,' translation of Muqadimatud-Dustur Aw al-Asbabul Mujibatulah, Article 184

[7] Ibid

[8] Taqiuddin an-Nabhani, 'The Islamic Personality,' Volume 2, translation of Shakhsiya Islamiyya, Dar ul-Ummah, Beirut, Fourth Edition, Chapter Al-Must'amin

[9] Taqiuddin an-Nabhani, 'The draft constitution of the Khilafah State,' Op.cit., Article 7f

[10] Taqiuddin an-Nabhani, 'The Islamic Personality,' Op.cit., Chapter Ahkam adh-*dhimmi*

[11] Narrated by Yahya b. Adam in the book of Al-Kharaaj

[12] Reported by al-Tabarani in Al-awsat on good authority

[13] Shaha al-Deen al-Qarafi, Al-furuq

[14] Bat Ye'or, 'The *Dhimmi*, Jews and Christians under Islam,' 1985 Associated University Presses, p. 56

[15] Holy Qur'an, Chapter 5, Surah al-Ma'idah, Verse 42

[16] Holy Qur'an, Chapter 5, Surah al-Ma'idah, Verse 106

[17] Ahmad ad-Da'our, 'The Rules of Testimonial Evidences,' Translation of Ahkaam al-bayyinaat, Chapter: Conditions (shuroot) of the witness

[18] Bat Ye'or, Op.cit., p. 57

[19] Narrated from Amru bin Shuaib from his father from his grandfather

[20] Al-Bayhaqi, extracted from the hadith of Abdurrahman Al-Bailimani

[21] Abdurrahman Al-Maliki, 'The Punishment System,' translation of Nidham ul-uqubat, Dar Ul-Ummah, Beirut, Second Edition, Chapter: Al-Qawad

[22] Cecil Roth, 'The House of Nasi: Dona Gracia'

[23] Abu 'Ubayd al-Qasim ibn Sallam, 'The Book of Revenue,' Translation of Kitab al-Amwal, Garnet Publishing Ltd, p. 42

[24] http://www.jews-for-allah.org/jewish-mythson-islam/*dhimmi*-tax-fiftypercent.htm

[25] Holy Qur'an, Chapter 9, Surah at-Taubah, Verse 29

[26] Taqiuddin an-Nabhani, 'The draft constitution of the Khilafah State,' Op.cit., Article 7a

[27] Abdul-Qadeem Zalloom, 'Funds in the Khilafah State,' translation of Al-Amwal fi Dowlat Al-Khilafah, Al-Khilafah Publications, 1988, p. 58

[28] Abu 'Ubayd, Op.cit., p. 25

[29] Ibid, p. 37

[30] Abdul-Qadeem Zalloom, Op.cit., p. 61

[31] Sahih Bukhari

[32] Narrated by Yahya b. Adam in the book of Al-Kharaaj

[33] Abu 'Ubayd, Op.cit., p. 37

[34] Taqiuddin an-Nabhani, 'The Ruling System in Islam,' Op.cit., 271

[35] Abu 'Ubayd, Op.cit., p. 40

[36] Sahih Bukhari

[37] Ibid, on the authority of Anas

[38] Thomas W. Arnold, 'The Preaching of Islam,' Second Edition, Kitab Bhavan Publishers, New Delhi, p. 128

[39] Ibid, p. 47

[40] Muhammad Asad, 'The Principles of State and Government in Islam,' Dar al-Andalus Ltd, Gibraltar, 1985, p. 41

[41] Holy Qur'an, Chapter 65, Surah at-Talaq, Verse 6

[42] Sahih Bukhari, narrated from Abu Hurairah

[43] Taqiuddin an-Nabhani, 'The Ruling System in Islam,' Op.cit., 235

[44] Ibid, p. 247

[45] Holy Qur'an, Chapter 2, Surah al-Baqarah, Verse 256

[46] Thomas W. Arnold, Op.cit., p. 47

[47] Abu 'Ubayd, Op.cit., p. 25

[48] Taqiuddin an-Nabhani, 'The Islamic Personality,' Op.cit., Chapter Ahkam adh-*dhimmi*

[49] Taqiuddin an-Nabhani, 'The draft constitution of the Khilafah State,' Op.cit., Articles 5&6

[50] Ibid

www.ingramcontent.com/pod-product-compliance
Lightning Source LLC
Chambersburg PA
CBHW062032280526
45787CB00005B/2291